The Pony Express
True Tales and Frontier Legends

Don't Miss a Single Adventure!
Read all the books in the Fields of Silver and Gold series.

#1 Sarah Winnemucca:
A Princess for the People

#2 Snowshoe Thompson:
Sierra Mailman

#3 Anne Martin:
The March for Suffrage

#4 Ben Palmer:
Black Pioneers on the Frontier

#5 The Pony Express:
True Tales and Frontier Legends

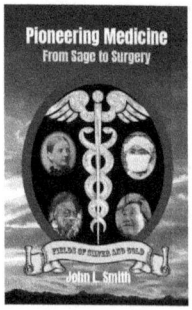

#6 Pioneering Medicine:
From Sage to Surgery

Find details at keystonecanyon.com

FIELDS OF SILVER AND GOLD

The Pony Express
True Tales and Frontier Legends

John L. Smith

KEYSTONE CANYON PRESS

Reno, NV

In memory of Robert Cassidy,
as brave as any pony rider

KEYSTONE CANYON PRESS

Publisher Alrica Goldstein
Copyeditor Paul Szydelko
Cover Designer Alissa Gates Booth
Photo Research/Proofread Caelin De Sa

Keystone Canyon Press
2341 Crestone Drive
Reno, NV 89523
www.keystonecanyon.com

Copyright © 2022 by John L. Smith

Images: Horse sillouhette by FreeVector.com, Dust Vectors by Vecteezy, Remaining images from LOC and Alrica Goldstein

All rights reserved. No part of this book may be reproduced in any manner whatsoever without written permission except in the case of brief quotations embodied in critical articles and reviews.

Library of Congress Control Number: 2022938877

ISBN 978-1-953055-20-0
EPUB ISBN 978-1-953055-21-7

Manufactured in the United States of America

Contents

- Author's Note vi
- Timeline vii
- Map of Pony Express Route viii
- April 3, 1860–October 24, 1861 ix
1. The "Swift Phantom of the Desert" Approaches .. 1
2. The Legend Begins 5
3. "Orphans Preferred" 15
4. From St. Joe to Sacramento, and Back Again – 1860 25
5. Pony Bob's Wild Ride 34
6. Hank Monk Takes the Reins 43
7. Did Buffalo Bill Ride for the Pony Express? ... 53
8. The Pony Rests, the Legend Lives On 61
9. One Last Ride with Pony Bob 66
- Glossary 70
- Key Characters 71
- Selected Bibliography and Further Reading ... 72
- Questions for Discussion 74
- Index 75
- About the Author 77

Author's Note

Historians prefer to use primary sources (letters, diaries, speeches, and photographs) to learn about historical events. Sometimes facts aren't written down as they happen so historians use secondary sources (things written about a historical event by someone who did not witness the event). With these pieces of information, they have to be critical thinkers that put the facts that they know together to make their best guess at what really happened.

You can be a critical thinker too! Keep reading about history that makes you think and dig deeper. Find new sources and think about how that might fit in with what you already know. Understanding our history helps us understand our world.

Timeline

1848 Gold discovered at Sutter's Mill in California.

1849 California gains statehood.

1851 George Chorpenning receives first contract to deliver the mail from Salt Lake City in Utah Territory over the Sierra to Sacramento, California. His "Jackass Mail" service takes up to fifty-four days.

1860 On January 27, Russell, Majors & Waddell freight company agrees to create a "pony express" relay to ensure a speedier delivery of important letters, documents, and news to the West.

1860 On April 3, the Pony Express begins its first run from St. Joseph, Missouri, to Sacramento.

1860 On June 16, the US Congress authorizes the secretary of the Department of Treasury to subsidize the building of the transcontinental telegraph.

1860 Pyramid Lake Indian War in Nevada temporarily halts Pony Express service during the summer.

1861–1865 American Civil War takes place.

1861 On October 26, with the telegraph completed, the Pony Express discontinues its service.

Map of Pony Express Route

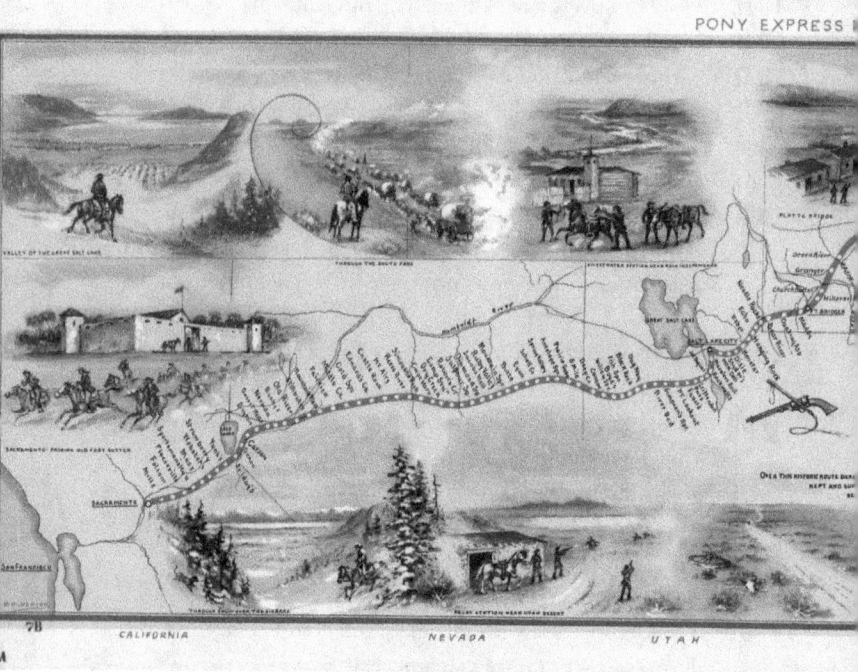

April 3, 1860—October 24, 1861

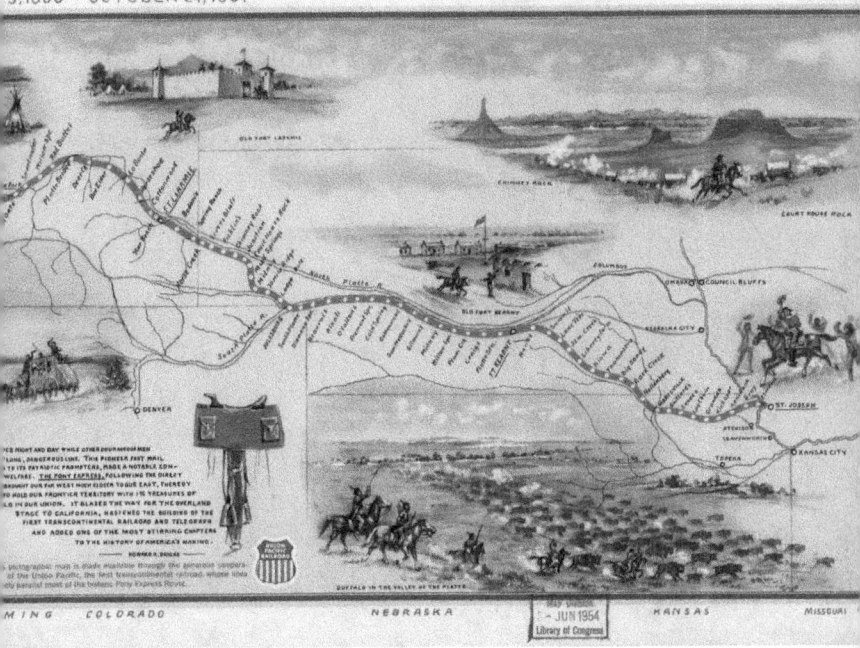

The pony-rider was usually a little bit of a man, brimful of spirit and endurance.

—Mark Twain, Roughing It

1

The "Swift Phantom of the Desert" Approaches

The Overland stagecoach rocked and rattled along the long and rutted road outside Scotts Bluff on the western edge of the Nebraska Territory. Out the windows, the Great Plains stretched in all directions. In the distance, Chimney Rock reached 480 feet above the rolling grasslands.

Atop the stage on the "box," as his seat was called, the driver handled the reins of six harnessed horses. Although exposed to the elements, the driver could spot friend and foe alike at a long distance from that vantage point.

Passengers inside the cramped coach struggled to find comfort and strained their eyes staring into the vast distance. One young man bound for Carson City, in what was to become Nevada, was especially fidgety. He joined the rest as they searched the horizon hoping to catch even a glimpse of a Pony Express rider as he raced across his rugged route. Although the speedy mail service

Chimney Rock towers over the Platte River Valley in Nebraska. It was a landmark stop on the Oregon Trail and dates back to the Oligocene Age.

was just a few months old, its intrepid riders had already captured the imagination of the public at a pivotal time in the growing nation's history. The young man contemplated his future in the West as he squinted for any sign of the rider, whom he would later describe as "the fleet messenger who sped across the continent." The Pony Express mail relay traveled roughly 1,966 miles from St. Joseph, Missouri, to Sacramento, California, in ten days or less. In 1860, that was lightning speed.

"Think of that for perishable horse and human flesh to do!" the traveler marveled. "The pony-rider was usually a little bit of a man, brimful of spirit and endurance. No matter what time of the day or night his watch came on, and no matter whether it was winter or summer, raining, snowing, hailing, or sleeting, or whether his 'beat' was level straight road or a crazy

Stagecoaches like this carried passengers loaded high with packages in all sorts of weather. The steel rimmed wheels felt every bump along the way.

trail over mountain crags and precipices, or whether it led through peaceful regions or regions that swarmed with hostile Indians, he must be always ready to leap into the saddle and be off like the wind!"

In good weather, a speeding stagecoach might travel 100 miles per day. That was several times faster than emigrant wagons pulled by a team of plodding oxen, but it was no match for the Pony Express riders. Their relay race covered 250 miles in the same time. The challenge for passengers confined to a relatively slow-moving stagecoach in such a big country was actually seeing one in action.

"We had had a consuming desire, from the beginning, to see a pony-rider, but somehow or other all

Mark Twain at 25 years old

that passed us and all that met us managed to streak by in the night, and so we heard only a whiz and a hail, and the swift phantom of the desert was gone before we could get our heads out of the windows," the traveler recalled. "But now we are expecting one along every moment, and would see him in broad daylight."

Suddenly, it happened. From his perch the driver shouted, "Here he comes!"

"Every neck is stretched further, and every eye strained wider," the traveler recalled years later. "Away across the endless dead level of the prairie a black speck appears against the sky, and it is plain that it moves. Well, I should think so! In a second or two it becomes a horse and rider, rising and falling, rising and falling—sweeping toward us nearer and nearer—growing more and more distinct, more and more sharply defined—nearer and still nearer, and the flutter of the hoofs come faintly to the ear . . ." And then, "a wave of the rider's hand, but no reply, and man and horse burst past our excited faces, and go winging away like a belated fragment of a storm!"

That young traveler, who would one day be known to the world as the great American writer Mark Twain, could scarcely believe his eyes.

2

The Legend Begins

Its official name was a real mouthful: The Central Overland California & Pikes Peak Express Company. It was better known as the Pony Express.

The Pony Express didn't last long—a little more than eighteen months. Nor was it profitable. It left the men who made it financially ruined. But from the morning of April 3, 1860, to the day the horses stopped running on October 26, 1861, it managed to carve out one of the most endearing and lasting legends in the history of the American West.

The legend of the Pony Express is so powerful, in fact, that it can be extremely difficult to separate fact from fiction. Over the years, the tales have grown taller with the telling as writers by the score have weighed in on the brief but colorful era.

Like the best legends, however, the amazing characters associated with the frontier mail service were real people who overcame great obstacles and accomplished remarkable things in their time in the saddle.

Statues like this one line the Pony Express route to celebrate these riders.

America's population, more than twenty-three million in 1850, was rapidly growing. Westward expansion came more slowly, even after the vast region was mapped. Communication was difficult, to say the least. Letters sent from the East often went by ship starting in the Atlantic Ocean down to Panama, where they were carried by mule and canoe across the marshy interior to the Pacific Ocean side and put on another ship to sail up to San Francisco. When President James K. Polk in 1845 sent a message to officials in California, it took six months to arrive!

Like so many developments in the West, our story really begins in 1848 with the discovery of gold at Sutter's Mill in California. News of the wealth to be had in the rivers, streams, and foothills of the Sierra

Mail was carried on steam ships that used both wind and steam to power them through the southern route before the Panama Canal was built.

Nevada range set off a rush of migration from the East. Although the population of the West was still quite small, emigrants seeking fertile farmland in Oregon and Washington and religious freedom in the Utah Territory were also moving in ever-increasing numbers. They came in wagons pulled by oxen, on horseback, and even on foot with all their belongings in a wooden handcart.

With a rapidly rising population—California's jumped from 92,597 in 1849 to 260,000 just three years later—it became necessary to improve the ability to communicate over long distance. In a time before the internet and telephone, it was a daunting challenge.

Even the telegraph, the machine that enabled long-distance communication by transmitting a series of coded electrical signals over a wire between two stations, did not yet reach all the way to the West Coast.

Like so many others, George Chorpenning Jr. came to California after the discovery of gold. He made a name for himself but not as a successful miner. He only achieved success after receiving a $14,000 annual contract with the US Post Office in 1851 to transport monthly mail between Sacramento and Salt Lake City in Utah Territory. He called it the "Jackass Mail" because of the mules and burros he used. It was a journey that meant crossing over the snow-capped Sierra Nevada range. It was considered the most difficult leg of the overland journey and averaged about thirty days from start to finish, but was unreliable and at the mercy of the weather. One trip took fifty-four days.

As newcomers flooded into lands that had long been home to indigenous tribes, it was also an increasingly dangerous time. In the autumn of 1851 at Stone House in what is now part of Humboldt County, Nevada, five men (including George's partner Captain Absolam Woodward) were killed in a fight with Shoshone Indians in a battle over control of their ancestral lands. Chorpenning continued to deliver the mail alone before changing to a safer and more passable route. Legendary Sierra mailman John "Snowshoe" Thompson filled that lapse in delivery in the winter.

Communication was essential leading up to the Civil War, and repairing telegraph lines that had been intentionally cut was labor intensive.

By 1858, the Butterfield Overland Mail Company was rolling from St. Louis to San Francisco on what it called the 2,800-mile "Oxbow Route." In good weather, and traveling around the clock, a Butterfield stage could go from St. Louis southwest through

Missouri and Arkansas into the wild lands that led to Texas, New Mexico, Arizona, and finally to California in twenty-five days. The mail got through, and the passengers held on for dear life.

With political turmoil in the Union and talk of the possibility of war between the states of the North and South over the complex issue of slavery, fast communication was more important than ever as the 1860 presidential election approached.

Historians differ about who first thought of the idea of the Pony Express. One person often credited is California senator William Gwin, who in 1859 made the acquaintance of an employee of a freight company owned by William Russell, Alexander Majors, and William Waddell. In the time before the railroad reached the West Coast, freight wagons pulled by slow-moving teams of strong Kentucky mules were the equivalent of today's long-haul tractor-trailers. It was recorded that the transport operation at one point used one thousand Kentucky mules and hundreds of their smaller cousins. They shipped goods and materials that were unavailable to the American frontier's growing population of emigrants.

Gwin wondered aloud whether riders on horseback carrying the mail might use the same routes to make speedy deliveries back and forth from California to St. Joseph, Missouri. Few knew the trail as well as the Russell, Majors & Waddell Company. When informed

Historians can tell a lot about how a structure was used by looking at the ruins. This building was the Cold Springs Station for the Pony Express.

of Gwin's goal, Russell jumped at the idea and agreed to start the "Pony Express" by spring. What's more, Russell also promised the mail service would be able to deliver a letter from St. Joseph to Sacramento in just ten days. Even taking a much straighter route than John Butterfield's mail stages, it was still a journey of nearly two thousand miles.

Truth be told, Russell, Majors & Waddell had suffered substantial losses from attacks on their wagon trains, some of which were burned. The men were in serious financial trouble and agreed to take on the job in part because they believed Gwin would help land them a federal contract that would make their

At swing stations, hostlers took in the exhausted horses and switched them out for fresh ones in a move that took just minutes.

efforts profitable. Although they were experienced, like so many frontier business entrepreneurs, Russell and his partners didn't fully realize the financial and physical risks involved. As poet Arthur Chapman sagely observed, "Men in the whirl of frontier activities seldom stopped to figure the costs. . . . Fantastic schemes lost all aspect of distortion. . . . The Pony Express could not have been born in any other era."

On January 27, 1860, Russell, Majors, and Waddell formed the Central Overland California & Pikes Peak Company (COC&PP). They immediately set to work mapping the best routes and hastily arranging for a long string of relay stations where riders could transfer quickly onto a fresh horse and home stations where they could rest after a long day in the saddle. The home stations, which included a blacksmith shop and provided a bed and a hot meal, were about 100 miles apart. Relay stations, known to the riders as "swing stations," were often crudely constructed of canvas or whatever materials were available. They were often no more than shacks made of stone, or dugouts that provided little protection from the weather or hostile attack. In all, 184 stations were designated.

Four hundred horses were purchased. Some of the best animals cost as much as $200 each—more than half-a-year's pay for an average cowboy. The animals had to be fast and durable. Men called hostlers were hired to care for the animals. Some station keepers brought their families along. Others maintained lonely outposts located miles from the nearest human being and a long day's ride from anything resembling a town.

Although less is known about the breed of animal used to fill the stations on the eastern half of the route, they were likely sturdy Morgan horses and possibly Thoroughbreds. Horses native to California and mixed-breed ponies were used for much of the western half of the journey. They were smaller than Thoroughbreds, but they were tough and durable and considered by observers to be "strong and full of spirit, remarkably free travelers, and possessing the most wonderful powers of endurance."

The Pony Express would use hundreds of horses in its brief existence, and the barely broken western animals came to symbolize the wild reputation of the endeavor. As Majors would write in his 1893 autobiography, "The horses were mostly half-breed California mustangs, as alert and energetic as their riders, and their part in the service—sure-footed and flee—was invaluable."

The animals would need every bit of strength to do their jobs. Within weeks, the corrals were full of well-fed and carefully selected horses.

After an investment estimated at $70,000, now all Russell, Majors, and Waddell had to do was find men brave enough to ride them.

3

"Orphans Preferred"

On March 19, 1860, an advertisement appeared in *The Sacramento Union* newspaper under the heading, "Men Wanted." It read, "The undersigned wishes to hire ten or a dozen men, familiar with the management of horses, as hostlers, or riders on the Overland Express Route via Salt Lake City. Wages $50 per month."

Even in those rough-and-tumble frontier days, finding capable riders for the Pony Express wasn't easy. After all, it wasn't a trail ride or even a speedy thoroughbred race. Nor was it like riding in an emigrant wagon train. Although a single rider would be responsible for only a part of it, it was an unpredictable journey that totaled nearly two thousand miles.

Riders would travel through lands where predators such as mountain lions, bears, and wolves were common. Where bison herds were present on the Great Plains, riders were advised to give the unpredictable animals a wide berth.

The dramatic increase of emigrants, settlers, ranchers, and prospectors increased tensions with

"Recovered from mail stolen by the Indians in 1860"

Native American tribes who struggled and sometimes fought to remain on their ancestral lands. In Nevada, the normally peaceful Northern Paiute tribe was about to go to war against the emigrants after being pushed from their hunting and gathering homeland.

In addition, there were the robbers, sometimes called "road agents," to consider. Lone riders were vulnerable to ambush. It was dangerous duty.

Riders had to be expert in the saddle, small in stature, but tough as cowhide. They needed to be as lightweight as possible and able to race at top speed across unpredictable land for hours at a time. They had to be able to withstand withering summer heat, blinding dust storms, monsoon rains, and winter blizzards too. It was not a job for the faint of heart.

In his memoir, Alexander Majors wrote, "Lightweights were deemed the most eligible for the purpose; the lighter the man the better for the horse, as some portions of the route had to be traversed at a speed of twenty miles an hour."

In an effort to recruit the right people for the job, a poster was printed to advertise the unique opportunity. It read:

> "WANTED – YOUNG, SKINNY WIRY FELLOWS NOT OVER EIGHTEEN. MUST BE EXPERT RIDERS, WILLING TO RISK DEATH DAILY. ORPHANS PREFERRED."

Like so many stories surrounding the Pony Express, even the authenticity of the colorful advertisement is in dispute. Despite the ominous tone—or perhaps because of it—there was no shortage of adventure-seekers who were, no doubt, also intrigued by the prospect of good pay. Riders were promised a monthly salary of up to $125—that's approximately $4,273 in 2022, accounting for inflation—with some receiving bonuses for literally going the extra mile.

Of the three owners of the company, Majors emerged as the driving force behind the Pony Express. His experience in the cross-country freight-shipping business, which brought supplies from the East to the settlers in the West, gave him a greater understanding of the route and the challenges the riders would face.

William Russell was a deeply religious man who did not drink alcohol. His personal beliefs were reflected in his hiring practices. He not only sought

In the end, only six riders died during the service: four were killed by native attacks and two froze to death.

riders of great skill and stamina, but he also wanted to recruit persons of high moral character. Bibles were distributed to riders when they were hired. They were also required to sign a pledge to the Central Overland California & Pikes Peak Express Company (COC&PP) promising to follow strict rules of behavior. It stated:

> "I _____, do hereby swear, before the Great and Living God, that during my engagement, and while I am an employee of Russell, Majors & Waddell, I will, under no circumstances, use profane language; that I will drink no intoxicating liquors; that I will not quarrel or fight with any other employee of the firm, and that in every respect I will conduct myself honestly, be faithful in my duties, and so direct all my acts as to win the confidence of my employers. So help me God."

It is necessary to add that riders commonly violated their pledge. Many stories have been written about their drinking, cursing, and fighting. They had chosen a dangerous road to travel.

Still, Majors would recall them fondly the rest of his life.

> "Not only were they remarkable for their lightness of weight and energy, but their service required continual vigilance, bravery and agility," he

wrote in his memoir. "Among their number were skillful guides, scouts, and couriers, accustomed to adventures and hardships on the plains—men of strong wills and wonderful powers of endurance."

They would have to be all that in their relay race against time. Starting from the east at St. Joseph, the route passed through modern-day Kansas, Nebraska, Colorado, Wyoming, Utah, Nevada, and finally to Sacramento, California. From there, the mail was transferred to a steamboat, where it made its way down the Sacramento River to San Francisco. The arrival of the Pony Express mail was then announced in the newspapers. Those who received letters would check the news, and if they saw their name on the list they would go to the Pony Express office and pick up their mail.

Imagine all that effort just to receive the mail. Russell, Majors & Waddell promised to deliver the mail in ten days—far less than half the time it took for stagecoaches to transport it.

The Pony Express was fast, but expensive. Letters crossed the country quickly, but sending them cost five dollars per one-half ounce. To save weight, the letters were written on tissue-thin paper. Even when it was running at full capacity, the price and space limitations made some people wonder whether the mail service would be financially successful.

The Pony Express was out of reach for average Americans due to the price of postage. It was so

Letters addressed to Carson City, Nevada had few ways to be delivered.

expensive that within a few months the price dropped all the way to one dollar per half-ounce letter. To give an idea of just how expensive that was, in 1860 the average hourly wage for laborers was just ten cents. Cowboys were paid an average of one dollar a day. Carpenters earned fourteen cents per hour, and blacksmiths eighteen cents per hour. For most, the cheapest way to send a letter was by the slower, but less expensive Overland Mail stagecoaches that took about twenty-four days to complete their run and cost about forty cents from California.

As the first run approached, every effort was made to save weight and time. St. Joseph saddle maker Israel Landis designed a racing-style saddle that weighed one-third of the traditional western

Mochila—Spanish for backpack—fit over the top of a saddle specially designed to be lightweight and easy to transfer.

saddle most riders used. Because the riders changed horses often during a single run, the mail was stored in a leather mochila that fit snuggly over the saddle but could quickly be removed and transferred to the fresh animal. Letters, telegrams, and documents sent by Pony Express were neatly placed into four leather pouches called cantinas attached to the mochila. After being stuffed with letters and telegrams, the cantinas were locked. When full, the mochila weighed about

This wood engraving from 1855 shows some of the territory that had to be crossed by the riders. There were estimated to be up to sixty million bison on the Great Plains in the early 1800s, but only 500 animals remained by 1900. Bison can weigh up to 2,200 pounds and are unpredictable.

ten pounds. The transfer of horses at the station took just two minutes.

Some riders carried rifles, others holstered pistols. With just a canteen of water, the Bible they were issued, and their Pony Express oath, they rode into the wild country. A weapon sometimes came in handy on the trail, but his horse was the rider's greatest defense against tribal attacks and robbers. The animals were more instinctual than some of their two-legged partners, and they were capable of outrunning trouble.

This was not just a long-distance delivery. This was a cross-country race at top speed, averaging ten miles-per-hour for mile after mile, around the clock for ten days. The express route varied depending on weather.

Some detours were made to avoid encountering hostile Native American tribes. Even buffalo herds, unpredictable and at times unruly, sometimes clogged the route in great numbers.

On April 3, 1860, with talk in Washington, DC, of the possibility of a civil war between northern and southern states, and a war out West with the Paiute tribe brewing, the Pony Express began its race against time.

4

From St. Joe to Sacramento, and Back Again – 1860

An excited crowd gathered on April 3 in St. Joseph, Missouri to watch history being made. Witnesses would recall buildings decorated for the occasion with American flags waving in the spring breeze. Those assembled listened to a lively brass band and passed the time looking to the east for signs of the approach of the *Missouri*, a special Hannibal & St. Joseph Railroad train whose wood-fired engine sent billows of smoke high into the air as it raced across "The Show-Me State" to make up for lost time.

Given the honor and responsibility of completing the final leg of a long journey that began in Washington, DC, the *Missouri* was transporting the first letters entrusted to the riders of the Pony Express—and it was running late.

The mail included eighty-five items in all, including a special edition of the *New York Herald* and *Tribune*

The mural "Pony Express," by Frank Albert Mechau, Jr., at the Ariel Rios Federal Building, Washington, D.C., was created in 1937 to depict the "dangers of mail delivery in an artistic depiction of shapes and contours." It is part of a series of works commissioned to serve not only as artistic interpretations of history, but also as catalysts for dialogue about the nature of public art and an artist's freedom of expression.

in miniature and a message of congratulations from President James Buchanan to Governor John G. Downey of California. After leaving the nation's capital, the mail went by messenger to New York and then to Detroit, where it had been delayed. By the time it reached Hannibal across the Mississippi River just inside the Missouri state line, it was hours behind schedule. So engineer Addison "Ad" Clark fired up the engine and let out the throttle, tearing down the tracks for more than 206 miles and setting a speed record in the process. History and the people of St. Joe didn't want to be kept waiting.

After three hours, the *Missouri* finally roared into the station.

Like so many things about the Pony Express, the identity of the first rider has been muddled almost from the start. In some histories, young J. W. "Billy" Richardson is the teenage rider credited. Others give the nod to Johnny Frye (sometimes spelled Fry.) Regardless, the rider got a late start. By the time the last speech was given and the cannon sendoff was fired, it was 7:15 p.m. The first rider was off on the shortest and safest jaunt of the entire trip, a few blocks down to the banks of the Missouri River, where a ferry waited to transport him across and into Kansas.

From there the race was on in earnest, changing horses every ten miles or so all the way to Nebraska, then briefly into Colorado, and again into Nebraska before going on to Wyoming. Mile after mile,

Strong boxes like the one here on the porch of the Pony Express Station in Placerville, CA kept mail and other valuables safe.

changing riders every seventy-five or one hundred miles, down through Utah and into Salt Lake City at 6:45 p.m. on April 9.

The rider rested, but the mail did not wait. A fresh horse and horseman headed west into the night toward Carson City and arrived in the future capital of Nevada at 2:30 p.m. on April 12. There was no time to waste.

The home stretch was almost in sight, but the hardest part of the journey was ahead: through the snowy Sierra Nevada and down into Placerville, then with William Hamilton in the saddle onward to Sacramento. At 5:45 p.m. on April 13, through streets lined with cheering residents, Hamilton made his way to the Alta Telegraph office for the first Pony Express delivery. He was right on time.

From there, the river steamboat *Antelope* brought the mail and the suddenly famous rider to the final destination in San Francisco.

It was met by a swarm of citizens celebrating in the streets, *The New York Times* reported, "with bands of music, fireworks were set off . . . the best feeling was manifested by everybody." Suddenly the great separation between the distant seat of American government in Washington, DC, and the farthest reaches of California didn't seem quite so extreme. The Pony Express delivered the mail, and with it a sense of unifying national pride at a time when America was in danger of being torn apart by civil war.

With that in mind, it's little wonder that its riders inspired so much admiration and respect.

The first run from Sacramento to St. Joseph was also momentous, but by now you've probably guessed the identity of the first rider is in dispute. Although he only made the steamboat cruise from San Francisco to Sacramento, it has been reported that James Randall was the first rider. But wouldn't you know that one Harry Roff, atop a "spirited half-breed bronco," is also credited with the first ride from the California state capital to Placerville with about fifty letters and telegrams in the mochila. Still, it makes sense that Hamilton was the first rider because Sacramento-to-Placerville was his section of the route. He is said to

Riders Billy Richardson and Johnny Frye (top), Charles and Gus Cliff (bottom).

have handed off the mochila to another historic rider named Warren Upson.

Although some of the names have blurred over time, the delivery of the first eastbound mail by Pony Express was made on time in ten days. The very idea was thought by many to be impossible.

The history of the Pony Express is loaded with stories of riders who possessed great endurance. One notable example was William "Bill" James, who was born in Virginia and came west to Utah Territory about the time Mormon pioneer Brigham Young led his followers on the long journey to the edge of the Great Salt Lake. In what is now Nevada, James rode across the high desert of Smoky Valley, along the Reese River, and over mountains that had long been home to the Shoshone tribe. According to one account, he favored riding mustangs and once made a 120-mile round trip in eight hours. That was lightning quick.

When it came to stamina and endurance, few riders could match Jack Keetley, a tough nineteen-year-old who was responsible for the run from Marysville, Kansas, to Big Sandy, Nebraska. He claimed to have ridden 340 miles, stopping only to change horses before falling asleep in the saddle! Keetley's feat is remembered in part because he wrote letters about his adventures in the Pony Express.

In his own remembrance of his time on the trail with the mail, J. G. Kelley recalled the terrible violence of the Pyramid Lake War between the Paiute and volunteer militia led by Major William Ormsby.

"As I look back on those times," Kelley said, "I often wonder that we were not all killed."

The job of operating the relay stations was by far the most dangerous duty on the route. The stations were by necessity set up in isolated areas far from the protection a town provided. Several riders did die from causes ranging from an attack by hostile Indians to freezing to death after getting lost in a blizzard.

One of the saddest tales is the fate of fourteen-year-old Billy Tate, who rode the Ruby Valley route in Nevada during the Paiute War. It has been recorded that he was attacked and fought bravely before being killed. As the story is told, he killed several of his adversaries before suffering fatal wounds and was not scalped as a sign of respect for his bravery in battle.

5

Pony Bob's Wild Ride

The Pony Express gained its legendary status despite its brief existence in part because of the endurance and heroism of the riders, many of whom were little more than children. Their stories of long rides in a hostile land printed in newspapers across the nation fed the public's romantic and often wildly inaccurate image of the West. The riders came to symbolize the intrepid independence, the overcoming of great obstacles, and fearless perseverance that Americans have long admired.

Robert Haslam, known to all as Pony Bob, just might have been the most famous rider of all. In a group known for its stamina and courage, he had few peers. Born in 1840 in London, he came to America as a teenager and sought prosperity in the West. Although fortune ultimately eluded him, he found fame on horseback after meeting Bolivar Roberts, a Pony Express superintendent in charge of most of Nevada and all of the California section of the route.

Stations like this one at Ft. Bridger in Wyoming allowed plenty of room to stable horses and provided places for the boys to eat and sleep between runs. Supervising a station was far more dangerous than riding for the Pony Express and quite a few stations were attacked or burned down. These stations were often built at critical water sources that the Indians relied on, causing further conflict.

After helping Roberts quickly construct some of the relay stations, Haslam was hired as a rider. At age twenty, he was among the older riders hired for the dangerous duty at a time of increasing tension between Carson Valley settlers and members of the Paiute tribe. He was assigned the run from Friday's Station at Lake Tahoe to Buckland's Station on the Carson River. It was a distance of about seventy-five miles. At top speed he descended from Lake Tahoe down to Genoa, north to Carson City, northeast to Dayton, then through a series of relay stations with names like

Miller's, Ragtown, Old River, Stillwater, and Mountain Well. Then came the last stretch to Buckland's, a home station where he could get a hot meal and rest up until it was time to retrace his route later in the week.

For a rider of Haslam's skill and stamina it was a fairly simple run, but those were not simple times. Violence continued to increase between the Northern Paiute and the settlers who continued to move into country the Indians had long called home. The "Numa," or "People," as they called themselves, saw the pinyon pine trees they relied on for food cut down for use as mining timbers for the silver mines of the Comstock Lode. Newcomers were taking their traditional game and grazing lands.

Settlers and Indians alike were victims of violence, but after the harsh winter of 1859 the Paiute had reached the point of desperation. On May 6, 1860, in retaliation for the kidnapping of two Paiute girls, Indians attacked and burned Williams Station, a combination stagecoach and Pony Express station that had a general store and a saloon. Three station workers, including the men responsible for kidnapping the children, were killed.

When news of the violence reached Carson and Genoa, the townsfolk reacted by assembling the local militia led by Major William Ormsby. The volunteers, 105 in all, were armed but poorly trained. When they encountered what they believed to be a small number of Northern Paiute near Pyramid Lake, they foolishly

Chief Numaga (left) and Major Ormsby (right) were both involved in what became known as the Pyramid Lake War.

followed the Indians into a narrow canyon, where more than 200 warriors led by Paiute war chief Numaga ambushed them. By the time the battle ended, seventy-six volunteers and Ormsby himself had died.

The Paiute War of 1860 didn't last long, but it made travel for the Pony Express riders very dangerous. Haslam's ride down from Friday's Station to Carson City was uneventful, but once there he noticed the townsfolk gathering and preparing for a possible attack by the Paiute. He rode on not knowing what trouble waited ahead.

His day got a little longer when he reached Miller's Station and found its corral empty and its fresh horses taken not by the Paiute, but by settlers as they prepared to battle the Paiute. He was still fifteen miles from Buckland's Station but managed to coax his weary animal to what he believed would be the end of a full day in the saddle.

He didn't know it yet, but his ride had just begun as he dismounted his exhausted horse at the home station.

Following the violence at Williams Station, rider Johnny (sometimes called Johnson) Richardson was so sufficiently concerned for his safety that he refused to take the reins for his regularly scheduled run from Buckland's east to Smith's Creek in the Nevada interior. The route cut right through the heart of Paiute tribal land at the worst possible time.

After being informed of Richardson's decision, Haslam was approached by a regional superintendent named Marley, who offered him a fifty-dollar cash bonus if he'd mount up and take on the other man's route. He didn't hesitate. With a fresh horse beneath him, he headed into the unknown. Pony Bob's wild ride was on!

He made the long gallop past the burned-out Williams Station, changed horses in Middlegate, then rumbled into the home station at Cold Springs (also called East Gate.) He wasn't finished. From there it was on to Edwards Creek station and at last to Smith's Creek, where he handed off his mochila to rider J. G. Kelley and rested for nine hours before loading a new mochila and returning to the trail with the westbound mail.

War with the Indians.
DETAILS OF THE FIGHT AT PYRAMID LAKE—PREPARATIONS FOR A VIGOROUS DEFENCE.

The Carson *Enterprise*, of the 15th ult., gives the following details of the recent fight at Pyramid Lake:

The different parties who were sent out to investigate the burning and murder at William's station, finding signs of Indians, organized and traced them to near Pyramid Lake. The force sent out consisting of the Carson City Rangers, Maj. Ormsby, Captain, the Genoa Rangers, under Capt. T. Condon, the Virginia Rangers, Capt. Archy McDonald, the Silver City Guards, Capt. R. G. Watkins, the whole force number 103 men, rank and file. The entire force was under the command of Maj. Ormsby.

On the morning of the 12th inst., the party struck the Big Meadows, on Truckee river, three miles from the lake. There they found a number of Indian warriors occupying a strong position on the hill to the right of the Meadows, about one-half mile in advance of the party. The command halted, and prepared for action; an order was given not to fire until the word was given. One man, while the company was forming, shot an Indian with a telescope rifle. The Indians then commenced firing on the party. The order was then given to charge. With three cheers the men charged up the hill, dispersing the foes, the Indians retreating until they got the whites in the position which suited them; they then commenced a murderous fire, killing a number of men; the whites still advancing on them. Then a party of Indians, who had succeeded in getting in the rear, commenced firing. The order was then to retreat to the original position in the Meadows. The retreat was orderly. Upon reaching the position, the order was to dismount and take to the timber. The Indians then commenced a galling fire on horses and men. The whites returned the fire until their ammunition

On June 12, 1860, *The New York Times* carried a story about the Pyramid Lake War. It used terms like "vigorous defence" and "murderous fire" that stirred up fear and hatred amongst its readers.

At Cold Springs, where he'd passed the previous day, a Paiute raid had resulted in the death of a station keeper and the theft of a corral full of fresh horses. Again he was riding on borrowed time as his animal began to tire. The next closest station was at Sand

Springs (sometimes called Mountain Well) more than twenty miles away. By the time he was back on a fresh horse, darkness had fallen. According to one account of his fateful ride, the darkness came in handy as he rode right past a Paiute war party.

Pony Bob retraced his tracks back to Buckland's and all the way up to Friday's Station. At 380 miles in less than forty hours, it was the longest ride in the history of the Pony Express. When the little Englishman was later asked about the record journey, he simply responded, "I was rather tired, but the excitement of the trip had braced me up to stand the journey."

Shortly after Haslam completed his run, the violence of the Paiute War halted Pony Express service for several weeks. By July, Fort Churchill was under construction near Buckland's Station and there was an increased military presence in the region. Completed in 1861, the fort served as an Army headquarters and a station for the Pony Express and Overland Mail stagecoaches.

When the Pony Express resumed its service, Haslam made his most important run but it wasn't the longest trip of his storied career. Haslam was part of the Pony Express relay that delivered the news of the election of Abraham Lincoln as America's sixteenth president in November 1860 and later transported a copy of the farewell address of outgoing president James Buchanan. It was a turning point in the nation's history. Beginning with South Carolina, eleven Southern states announced they were withdrawing from the United States of America and forming the Confederate States of America.

Lincoln believed slavery, although then legal, was morally wrong. Torn apart by the issue of slavery in the rest of the country and the secession of the Confederate States from the Union, the nation prepared for the likelihood of civil war. Americans who lived west of Missouri often had to wait weeks and even months to receive news of developments in Washington, DC. Tensions between the North and the South increased the possibility that new territories and states in the West, especially gold-rich California, might join the Confederacy.

That made the delivery of Lincoln's first inaugural address to the nation profoundly important, and Haslam and his fellow Pony Express riders delivered it on horseback in record time: seven days, seventeen hours.

Pony Bob's part was the most dangerous of all— 120 miles through hostile territory. Unlike his record-setting ride a few months earlier, he couldn't outrun trouble this time. With a copy of Lincoln's inaugural address in his mochila, he galloped at top speed only to be attacked by Paiute braves on horseback. Their arrows struck Haslam in the arm and face, breaking his jaw and dislodging five teeth.

If he failed, not only would he lose his life, but Californians and Nevadans might have to wait many more weeks before learning of the president's vision for America at a critical time.

Somehow, Haslam managed to remain in the saddle. After about four miles, the Paiute riders fell back and Pony Bob rode on. He completed his run to Fort Churchill in a record eight hours. While he was being treated for his wounds, the inaugural address was transmitted by Fred Bee's newly installed telegraph "Bee's Grapevine Line" that went over the Sierra Nevada using trees in the forest as its poles.

Lincoln's address was a measured call for patience and understanding even as the issue of slavery divided the country and brought its people to a war between the states.

Lincoln concluded with lines that echoed across the land and our history:

> "We are not enemies, but friends. We must not be enemies. Though passion may have strained, it must not break our bonds of affection. The mystic chords of memory, stretching from every battlefield and patriot grave to every living heart and hearthstone all over this broad land, will yet swell the chorus of the Union, when again touched, as surely they will be, by the better angels of our nature."

6

Hank Monk Takes the Reins

The riders of the Pony Express moved the mail across country at a gallop, but throngs of travelers longed to see the West for themselves. Whether seeking fortunes in the fields of silver and gold in Nevada and California, or, respectively, looking for a fresh start in the wide-open territory that appeared to offer unlimited possibilities, they yearned to be there.

But how?

Emigrant wagon trains pulled by oxen or mules took at least three months to travel from Missouri to Salt Lake City in the best of weather. Plans for a transcontinental railroad remained a dream on a drawing board.

That left the jarring but speedier horse-drawn wagons of the Butterfield Overland Mail and the Wells, Fargo & Co. stagecoaches, whose drivers carried passengers, mail, merchandise, and even large sums of gold across hundreds of miles of rugged

The transcontinental railroad was completed on May 10, 1869 at Promontory Summit, Utah. It connected the existing rail system in Council Bluffs, IA with the Oakland Long Wharf on San Francisco Bay.

terrain. As the red stages operated by Henry Wells and William G. Fargo came to dominate the route, by 1867 the company advertised travel from Sacramento, California, to Omaha, Nebraska, in just fifteen days.

The Wells Fargo Concord Coach, made by the Abbot-Downing factory of Concord, New Hampshire, was considered the sleekest and most comfortable vehicle of its era. It weighed 2,500 pounds and cost $1,100 to build. Three pairs of strong, durable, crossbred draft and quarter horses powered the stages.

The coaches stopped every ten miles or so at stations to change teams of horses. In minutes they

The Wells Fargo Coach was innovative for its time. The front wheels were smaller than the rear wheels so that it could make tighter turns and the spokes, made of hand-hewn hickory, were carved to ensure that they would flex under the load.

were off again, keeping to a schedule that barely gave passengers a moment's rest from the jarring and rocking of the wagon over primitive dirt roads.

It is important to remember that stage drivers were highly regarded and respected for their skill and courage. And when it came to skill as a driver and the ability to tell a grand story—something almost as important in the early West—Henry James "Hank" Monk was positively peerless.

Like so many people who made their mark in the frontier West, Monk started on the road early in life. Born in Waddington, New York, not far from the St.

Lawrence River, he grew up around horse-drawn wagons and took to driving them at an early age. By the time he was twelve, as the story is told, he was skilled with the reins and was hired to drive a stagecoach between two towns in northern New York. After gold was discovered in California, he chased his fortunes west in 1852. Ironically, he didn't arrive by stage, but sailed down to Panama, where he crossed the Isthmas on foot, reboarded a steamer and arrived in San Francisco.

In Sacramento, at age twenty-three, he first found work as a driver in Auburn for James Birch of the California Stage Company. At one time, Birch and his partner Frank Stevens controlled 80 percent of the stage lines in California long before it was better known for its crowded freeways.

Monk's expertise made him a valuable employee. His ability with the animals led to routes farther into the Sierras, where he drove from Sacramento to Placerville for the California Stage. After a few seasons, he knew every inch of the way and had gained a reputation as a top driver. He became known as the "Knight of the Lash" and the "King of Coachmen."

By 1857, he took the reins for the Overland Stage Company on the eastern slope of the Sierras. The route between Genoa and Placerville and up to Lake Tahoe suited him, and he moved into the St. Charles Hotel in Carson City, eventually driving for the Pioneer Stage Company, which eventually became a part of Wells, Fargo & Co.

Monk didn't get rich in the gold fields of California and Nevada, but he found national fame atop the Wells Fargo stage led by six harnessed horses that ran between Carson City and the gold-mining town of Placerville across the state line in California.

Like so many of his friends and acquaintances in that time before the easy entertainment of radio and television, he became an accomplished storyteller in saloons and station houses. His reputation as a daring driver grew rapidly. He was such a character that he was able to charge passengers on his stage as much as twenty dollars extra just to sit with him while he told his stories and worked his magic with the animals. Monk backed up his tales with a rare ability with the reins, which drivers sometimes called "the ribbons."

When he arrived at his destination, that's when the fun really began. Monk met Pony Bob in 1863, and they remained friends for many years. Haslam described Monk as a fit fellow with black hair and blue eyes. While working he wore the driver's traditional garb, including a long black duster coat and black boots. He carried a bullwhip and a pistol for protection. When he was finished for the night, he often changed out of his dust-covered clothing and into a clean suit of clothes. He lived up to the image of a daring and courageous stage driver.

Nellie Mighels Davis, perhaps Nevada's first woman newspaper reporter, recalled the thrill of riding at breakneck speed with Monk on the stage to Carson City.

Many other writers, including Dan DeQuille and Mark Twain, told tales—some of them pretty tall—about Monk's skill and ability to race his stage along narrow and winding mountain roads next to steep drop-offs. One mistake would mean certain injury or death.

Calling her meeting with the famous storytelling Nevada stage driver nothing less than a "dream come true," early Nevada writer Idah Meacham Strobridge captured a common sentiment about the famous tale-telling stage driver in her 1909 book *The Land of Purple Shadows:* "Hank Monk, the incomparable! The most daring—the most reckless of drivers; and the luckiest. The oddest, the drollest of all the whimsical characters who made Western staging famous the world over. . . . I'm quite sure that had anyone asked me which of the two I would rather see—hear—speak to, Hank Monk, or the President (and that I mean Abraham Lincoln), it would have been the former I unhesitantly would have chosen. Without a doubt my youthful judgment was bias, but the fact remains."

Monk's friend Pony Bob recalled the driver always traveling heavily armed for protection of himself, his passengers, and cargo. "Monk was only robbed once, and that time four men got the drop on him with shotguns," Haslam told a reporter. "They got about twenty-two thousand dollars in money and jewels. One of them was the foreman of the company's stable, and put the others on the job. Although the robbers were four to one, the robbery was always a sore subject to Monk."

Mark Twain tells the story in *Roughing It* of Hank Monk (left) driving Horace Greeley (right) from Carson City, NV to Placervile, CA.

Of all the tales Monk told and those that were told about him, the most famous of all is the story of how on July 30, 1859, he transported famous *New York Tribune* newspaper editor Horace Greeley from Genoa over the Sierra Nevada to Placerville to get him on time to a "grand dinner speech" he had scheduled. Greeley was a politically and socially influential speaker and writer who called for the settlement of the West and promoted the plan for a transcontinental railroad that would connect Americans on both coasts. He became famous for writing, "Go West, young man, and grow up with the country." He was considered a very important person, and people came from miles around to hear him.

Like so many citizens of the East, Greeley was intensely curious about the West. In 1859, the only practical way to reach California overland was by stagecoach. That's how he eventually met Monk in Genoa and told him he was running late for his speech.

In no time he found himself departing Genoa, bouncing around over a dirt road into the foothills of the Sierra Nevada with Monk on the box and handling the ribbons.

"I'll get you there!" Monk called out.

But the faster he drove his team of six, the bumpier the ride became. And, so, Greeley began to bounce around inside the coach. Back and forth, to and fro, side to side, up and down, he rattled around the coach like a pinball.

Although it was a few months before the start of the Pony Express, in a newspaper account, Monk's friend Haslam remembered being on the road that day. At a brief stop to water the horses, Haslam rode up and shouted, "You are moving them, Hank!"

The thoroughly rattled Greeley was not convinced Monk could complete the run in time for his 5 p.m. appearance. He considered pausing to send a telegram ahead to tell the crowd in Placerville he would be late, but the stage roared past the last telegraph station on the trail. The coach moved on at top speed and perilously close to disaster.

In an interview late in his life, Monk laughed at the memory.

"I looked into the coach and there was Greeley, his bare head bobbing, sometimes on the back and then on the front of the seat, sometimes in the couch and then out, and then on top and then on the bottom, holding on to whatever he could grab," he recalled.

During the wild ride, Monk supposedly told the newspaper editor, "Horace, keep your seat! I told you I would get there by five o'clock, and by God I'll do it, if the axles hold!"

Fortunately, the wheels did not fall off the coach. Monk delivered Greeley, shaken but unbroken, on time to the welcoming group that had assembled to hear him speak. Before Greeley returned to Genoa at a slower and safer pace, it was reported that he bought the driver a new suit.

And there the story might have ended had Greeley not been so impressed by the adventure and the skill of his driver that he sent a story about the trip by telegram to his newspaper. From there it took off and spread across the country. Newspaper after newspaper picked up the tale of the raucous journey of the esteemed editor and political influencer.

The story was considered such a grand tale that it was used as material by America's greatest humorist of the West in those days, Artemus Ward. When Mark Twain recounted the ride in his 1872 book *Roughing It*, the tale grew once more.

Monk said he also received from Greeley a gold pocket watch on a long chain, which he wore with pride and often showed his friends and fans between stories at the saloons he frequented. For the rest of his

life, Monk entertained passengers and passersby with his tales from riding tall on the box. He also regaled his friends with tales of driving other famous passengers, including President Rutherford B. Hayes, General William Tecumseh Sherman of the Union Army, and many singers and entertainers of the day.

By 1883, the era of the stagecoach was fading fast. His health and prosperity behind him, years of hard driving and hard living caught up with Hank Monk. He died of pneumonia on February 28. His death symbolized the end of an era of travel in the once very wild West.

Monk is buried in the Lone Mountain Cemetery in Carson City. His weathered headstone (above) was replaced by Gardnerville casino owner Sharkey Begovich, a character in his own right, and reads, "Most noted and celebrated stage driver in the West."

Considering Monk's wild life and times, those words sound almost understated.

7

Did Buffalo Bill Ride for the Pony Express?

William Frederick Cody, known to the world as "Buffalo Bill," is the most famous Pony Express rider of all. But a mystery surrounds his employment. There's no record of him working for the express, and some historians believe that Buffalo Bill wasn't a rider at all.

What is not in doubt is his status as a colorful character whose life became the stuff of legend, in part because he was a great storyteller and a marvelous showman. One thing is certain: he sure packed a lot of adventure into one lifetime.

Born on February 26, 1846, near LeClaire, Iowa, young Cody worked as a horse wrangler and messenger in Kansas for the freight company owned by Russell, Majors, and Waddell. After gold was discovered in 1859 in Colorado, Cody decided to seek his fortune there. According to one version of events, he learned

William Frederick "Buffalo Bill" Cody
(1846-1917)

that the new Pony Express was hiring "skinny, expert riders willing to risk death daily" and decided to apply for a job at a company owned by Russell, Majors, and Waddell. He was just 14 years old.

If he did ride for the Pony Express, he would have been among the youngest in the saddle. The records aren't clear about the precise identity of all eighty or so riders hired.

The legend of the Pony Express was so popular that men of its generation sometimes inserted themselves into stories about taking daring riders across dangerous lands, "with the tales of reckless adventure growing taller with the telling," as one Smithsonian National Postal Museum researcher put it. One of those, it appears, was "Broncho Charlie" Miller, who reportedly lived to 105 and claimed to have been the youngest, and last of the Pony Express riders. He swore he'd ridden for the service at age eleven and told his tales so authentically that two generations of

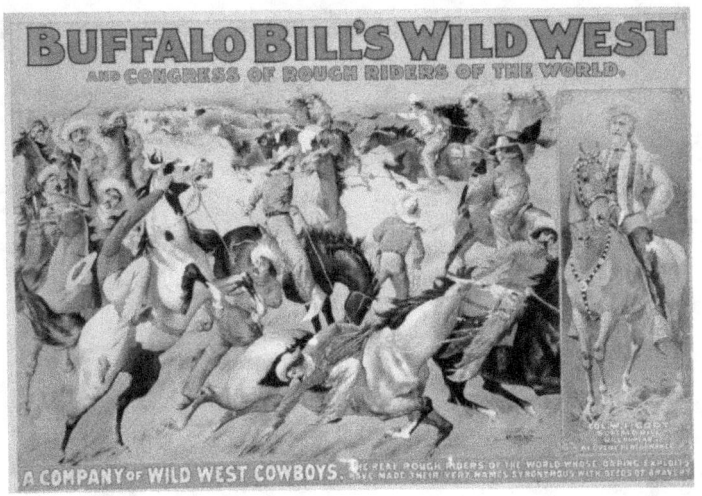

Poster advertising *Buffalo Bill's Wild West and Congress of Rough Riders of the World* show in 1899.

newspaper reporters believed him. The only record of a Charlie Miller in the Pony Express is one who had died long before the legend of Broncho Charlie was born. But wouldn't you know it, it appears he was acquainted with Buffalo Bill.

Bill Cody's life and exploits, real and embellished, were made wildly popular in part by the writer and promoter Ned Buntline through inexpensive "dime novels" and a play starring Buffalo Bill called *Scouts of the Plains*. It featured many pretend gunfights and actors portraying cowboys, gunfighters, hostile tribes, and a romance between Buffalo Bill and the Indian maiden Dove Eye. Opening in 1872 in New York, the show was poorly written and savaged by reviewers, but loved by people hungry for the flavor of a western most had never seen. It played to capacity audiences.

When Buffalo Bill literally took his own show on the road, he gained international celebrity and at one time was one of the best-known Americans. He was an excellent horseman and marksman, and *Buffalo Bill's Wild West and Congress of Rough Riders of the World* was an enormous circus-style show with nonstop action and real cowboys and Indians, trick riders, gunfight reenactments and exotically dressed Native Americans. The sharpshooter Annie Oakley was featured, and for one season Sioux Chief Sitting Bull made an appearance. Traveling by train, at one point the show employed ninety members of the Sioux and Pawnee Tribes and presented trick-shot artists galore. It used two hundred horses and offered city audiences a glimpse at real buffalo, bears, and elk.

Indian battles, gunfights with desperados, and the popular tale of the Pony Express were re-created under a big tent before excited audiences across America and Europe for more than thirty years.

Buffalo Bill became a legend, and the image of the Pony Express burned in the imaginations of a generation of people, many of whom had never traveled west, seen a buffalo in the wild, or even ridden a horse.

To this day, it's almost impossible to separate Cody's actual life from the tales he told to the world. "His claims of life as a Pony Express rider made

Annie Oakley began hunting at age 8 to support her impoverished family and won her first sharpshooting competition at age 15. Viewers of *Buffalo Bill's Wild West* show were delighted to see her split a playing card edge-on at 30 paces. After a rail accident left her disabled, she taught other women self-defense techniques. The Broadway musical *Annie Get Your Gun* is loosely based on her life.

for great theater," the Smithsonian notes, "but little accuracy." That has not dampened their almost universal appeal.

There is, however, another view of Cody's Pony Express status that was, at least in part, endorsed by Alexander Majors in his autobiography. Majors recalled young Cody as a boy of perhaps just nine years old working with the horses and mules and helping with the freight wagons. In the spring of 1860, Cody was assigned to ride a forty-five-mile section of the long relay. It's also true that Cody is responsible for getting Majors's book published.

Other stories of Cody's courage on the Pony Express trail are even harder to verify, but remain worth telling. He was credited with completing an exhausting 300-mile round-trip ride through the wilds of Wyoming, a marathon made necessary after his relief riders failed in their duty. The run, as the story is told, ended after twenty-two hours.

On another Wyoming run, again not possible to prove absolutely, Cody is said to have been chased by Sioux warriors to Three Crossings Station, where he discovered the station keeper dead and the corral empty of relief horses. He rode on to the next station, legend has it, where he convinced several men to join him in an effort to recover the horses, which had been stolen.

Cody served in the American Civil War as an Indian scout and later as a soldier in the Union Army's Seventh Kansas Cavalry. After the war, he hunted

This plaque by Buffalo Bill's grave in Colorado celebrated the centennial of the Pony Express.

buffalo to feed workers during the construction of the Union Pacific Railroad. He gained the nickname "Buffalo Bill" after reportedly killing more than four thousand animals.

He also continued to serve as an Army scout and hunting guide. As a scout, he was known for his courage and was awarded the Congressional Medal of Honor in 1872. His and hundreds of others medals were revoked after Congress retroactively tightened the rules for the honor in 1917, coincidentally the same year as Cody's death on January 10. The US Army reinstated the medals seventy-two years later.

For all that courageous living, he is probably best known as an entertainer who for forty-five years told the story of the American frontier to popular audiences. He always called himself an old Pony Express rider, although he was likely just a messenger.

Mark Twain counted himself among Buffalo Bill's many admirers and once wrote him a fan letter. "I have seen your Wild West show two days in succession, and I have enjoyed it thoroughly" the great writer and author of *The Adventures of Huckleberry Finn* said. "It brought vividly back the breezy wild life of the Great Plains and the Rocky Mountains, and stirred me like a war-song. Down to its smallest details, the show is genuine—cowboys, vaqueros, Indians, stage coach, costumes and all."

Like the show itself, the Pony Express was both real and imagined.

In *The Lives and Legends of Buffalo Bill*, author Don Russell acknowledges the possibility Cody's claim of being employed by the Pony Express might have been more brag than fact, but he wisely observes, "It is highly unlikely that the Pony Express would be so well remembered had not Buffalo Bill so glamorized it."

8

The Pony Rests, the Legend Lives On

On October 26, 1861, the Pony Express service that had captured the nation's imagination and managed to distract it for a while from the grim tragedy of the American Civil War, made its final cross-country run. In the farthest and wildest parts of the West way out in Nevada, riders still delivered mail on horseback and by wagon for several more years with other companies created to serve the isolated mining districts and ranching communities far from civilization and the nearest telegraph office.

The completion of the first transcontinental telegraph line that year made the Pony Express obsolete, but a strange thing happened after the dust from the last official ride settled. The legend of the Pony Express took on a life of its own. Thanks in no small part to the entertaining style of Buffalo Bill and the literary excesses of Ned Buntline and a generation of writers, the Pony Express grew in the nation's imagination and in the history of the West.

During its brief life, the Pony Express traveled 616,000 miles in total. It carried almost 35,000 pieces of mail and documents important to the history of the nation. It enabled news of elections, battles, and, tragically, the lists of those killed in the American Civil War to quickly reach the farthest edge of the settled West.

The Pony Express wasn't successful, but it was cherished as a reminder of America's common belief in self-reliance and courage on the frontier. As *California Pacific* magazine cheered in 1861, "We have looked to you as those who wait for morning, and how seldom did you fail us!"

A few months later, the hoofbeats were silent.

The nation's newspapers printed colorful stories and editorials that sang the praises of the brave riders and their animals even as they rode off into the sunset. The *Sacramento Bee's* adoring coverage was typical of many. It wrote, "Farewell Pony: Our little friend, the Pony is to run no more. . . . Farewell and forever, thou staunch, wilderness-overcoming, swift-footed messenger. For the good thou has done we praise thee; and, having run thy race, and accomplished all that was hoped for and expected, we can part with thy services without regret."

Russell, Majors, and Waddell would never forget their unwise decision to enter into an expensive business proposition without a contract. It left the three men in financial ruins. By one account, their company was $400,000 in debt when it closed its doors. Although the company initially received five dollars per ounce of mail carried, it lost money on every ride and as much as thirty

Monuments like this one in Sidney, NE kept the story of the Pony Express fresh in people's minds.

dollars on every letter it delivered, according to the Postal Museum. In the end, Russell, Majors, and Waddell saw a federal contract awarded to a rival company.

That didn't stop the legend from growing and becoming "hopelessly scrambled," as one writer put it. It became a point of pride to claim to have ridden for the Pony Express. Dozens of books, many inaccurate, were written on the subject. The heroics of the Pony Express riders, real and imagined, became a popular theme for radio shows and movies. Towns located more or less along the riders' routes placed markers memorializing their community ties to those brave mail carriers on horseback.

Stamp issued by the US Postal Service for the 100th anniversary in 1960.

Today, the Pony Express National Historic Trail is marked with plaques, signs, and memorials, and it stretches nearly two thousand miles from Missouri to California. It is administered by the National Park Service, which estimates that as many as fifty Pony Express stations or their remnants may one day be available to the public. What's more, two dozen museums are dedicated to the history and legend of the riders. Although the precise location of some home and relay stations has been difficult to determine, many efforts have been made to preserve what remains. Annual trail rides, some sponsored by the nonprofit National Pony Express Association, take place along the undeveloped stretches of the route where once horse and rider crossed the country in a cloud of dust.

The Pony Express wasn't alone in being left behind in rapidly changing times. The stagecoach era suffered a similar fate. With the completion of the Transcontinental Railroad on May 10, 1869, at Promontory, Utah, by the Union Pacific Railroad and Central Pacific Railroad companies, Americans could travel in relative comfort from the East all the way to California. Stage and mule-drawn freight lines steadily faded from use over the next three decades. By the early 1900s, they vanished from all but the most remote locations of the West. With the invention of the motorized vehicle, and the development of the motor bus, the stagecoaches that Hank Monk and his fellow drivers had handled so expertly were a thing of the past.

For all its faults, brief history, and blustery romance, the Pony Express will always be remembered as a brave business endeavor on the frontier. As the National Pony Express Association observes, "In the era before easy mass communication, the Pony Express was the thread that tied East to West."

9

One Last Ride with Pony Bob

The citizens of Nevada were back to business as usual in July 1868. The American Civil War had ended three years earlier. The Union had been saved, but the fighting between the North and South had taken a terrible toll on the nation. A long, painful healing process had begun. In Nevada, the mines of the Comstock Lode bustled with activity.

And the bosses of the rival Wells, Fargo & Co. and Pacific Union Express service decided to have a friendly competition to kick off the Independence Day celebration by staging a twenty-two-mile horse race between Reno and Virginia City with the winner receiving bragging rights.

The event brought to mind the not-so-distant past when the Pony Express riders galloped through on their way to Sacramento. The competitors brought the fastest horses and prepared weeks in advance of the big race. Excitement built throughout the communities, and by race day more than three

The Wells Fargo Express office in Virginia City, NV was the finish line to the race.

thousand people had crowded into Virginia City to take it all in. There was much speculation on the outcome and plenty of betting.

As always, Virginia City's major newspaper *The Enterprise* had a reporter on the scene to describe the event in excited detail. A challenge between two transportation companies in friendly competition during a time of celebration of America's Independence Day was transformed into a colorful and dramatic showdown.

And Bob Haslam once again found himself on horseback for the "grand race" between Wells, Fargo & Co. and the Pacific Union Express Company. Although no longer a reed-slim teenager—by 1868, he was the mature age of 28—Haslam weighed just 130 pounds. In the other saddle was a younger man named Frank Henderson, who weighed 139 pounds.

The match was designed for two riders galloping head-to-head, but others decided to join the fun. A buckboard driver named Bennett, who like Haslam also worked for Wells, Fargo & Co., decided to enter his "lightning express wagon" drawn by two fast horses into the race. He also positioned fresh horses along the race route, and managed to change them with remarkable precision, losing little time to the men on horseback. An excited reporter wrote that Bennett "came very near to beating both pony lines."

For a reason not explained, Bennett left Reno five minutes after the others but gained on them quickly— especially on the flat ground of the Truckee Meadows, but by Steamboat Creek his horses tired and stopped running. Changing horses, he was back in the race and again gained ground, reaching the top of the hill overlooking Virginia City—just six miles from the finish line and just two minutes behind the leaders!

Then Bennett and his wagon experienced in 1868 something modern automobile drivers sometimes experience, a "traffic" delay and detour caused by an accident. Up ahead in the dirt road, a large hay wagon pulled by teams of mules had overturned. Bennett was forced to take an alternate route that sent him one-half-mile off course. "With all this delay and disadvantage of one team giving out," a reporter wrote, "he arrived in Virginia City but twenty-five minutes behind Pony Bob."

There was another rider in the race, one who didn't start with the others but planned to finish ahead of them just to bring laughter to the thousands in attendance. After it became clear that Henderson could not catch Pony Bob, Mathew Bean entered the event from just outside of Virginia City and to everyone's surprise came storming at a full gallop on a fresh horse to thunderous applause. Instead of mail pouches, Bean carried gunny sacks filled with rolled-up *San Francisco Bulletin* newspapers. "He delivered the newspapers," one journalist reported, "and the crowd had a good laugh at the deception."

The real race was barely a race at all. Pony Bob caught Henderson quickly and increased the distance between them, arriving in Virginia City two miles ahead of the competition. His time: One hour, four minutes over a twenty-two-mile route.

Just like his heyday on the Pony Express, the legend on horseback was impossible to beat.

Glossary

Box: The driver's seat of a stagecoach.

Bronco: A wild horse, sometimes also called a mustang, still found in great numbers in Nevada. They were commonly used by Pony Express riders in the West, especially on the challenging run from Salt Lake City, Utah Territory, to Sacramento, California.

Cantinas: On a mochila, they are the locked pouches that contained letters and documents.

Emigrant: A person who leaves their own country to settle permanently in another.

Hostler: A person hired to groom and care for horses.

Immigrant: A person who comes to live permanently in a foreign country.

Mochila: The square leather saddle cover used by Pony Express riders to carry the mail.

Morgan: A sturdy breed of horse, one of the earliest breeds in America.

Oxbow Route: The long, looping route taken from St. Louis to San Francisco by the Butterfield Overland Mail Company.

Northern Paiute: One of the major tribes of Native Americans in Nevada, along with the Washoe, Western Shoshone, and Southern Paiute.

Shoshone: A Native American tribe generally located in Northern Nevada and Southern Idaho.

Telegraph: A machine capable of communicating messages by tapping a series of coded dots and dashes over an electrified wire.

Thoroughbred: A breed of horses known for their speed and ability.

Transcontinental: Across the continent.

Key Characters

William "Buffalo Bill" Frederick Cody: An American soldier, buffalo hunter, and showman who spread excitement and interest in the Pony Express through his Wild West shows.

George Chorpenning, Jr: An early pioneer of mail transport between Salt Lake City and Sacramento, CA. which took up to fifty-four days.

Horace Greeley: American newspaper editor and publisher of the New-York Tribune that popularized the slogan "Go West, young man, and grow up with the country."

William Gwin: One of California's first US Senators that may have been the person who suggested the idea of the Pony Express.

Robert "Pony Bob" Haslam: Pony Express rider credited with completing a 380-mile trip, the longest on record.

Alexander Majors: A partner of Russel and Waddell, Majors was responsible for mapping the trail of the Pony Express.

Henry James "Hank" Monk: Stagecoach driver responsible for transporting Horace Greeley from Carson City, NV to Placerville, CA.

Annie Oakley: Female sharpshooter that starred in Buffalo Bill's Wild West shows.

William Hepburn Russell: Business partner of Russell, Majors, and Waddell that set the moral tone and promised the deliver the mail in ten days.

Mark Twain: An American writer of humorous stories.

Selected Bibliography and Further Reading

Burton, Richard Francis. Fawn Brodie, Ed. *The City of the Saints and Across the Rocky Mountains to California.* New York: Alfred A Knopf, 1963.

Bloss, Roy. *Pony Express: The Great Gamble.* Berkeley, CA: Howell-North Books, 1959.

Bricklin, Julia. *The Notorious Life of Ned Buntline: A Tale of Murder, Betrayal, and the Creation of Buffalo Bill.* Lanham, MD: The Rowman and Littlefield Publishing Group, 2020

Carter, Robert A. *Buffalo Bill Cody: The Man Behind the Legend.* New York: John Wiley & Sons, 2000.

Chapman, Arthur. *The Pony Express: The Record of a Romantic Adventure in Business.* New York: G. P. Putnam's Sons, 1932.

Charles River Editors. *The Pony Express: The History and Legacy of America's Most Famous Mail Service.* Amazon Services, LLC, 2013.

Cody, William F. *The Life of the Hon. William F. Cody, Known as Buffalo Bill.* New York: Indian Head Books, 1991.

Corbett, Christopher. *Orphans Preferred: The Twisted Truth and Lasting Legend of the Pony Express.* New York: Broadway Books, 2003.

Dangberg, Grace. *Carson Valley: Historical Sketches of Nevada's First Settlement.* Carson City, NV: The Carson Valley Historical Society, 1972.

DeQuille, Dan (William Wright.) *The Big Bonanza: The Authentic Account of the Discovery, History and Working of the World-Renowned Comstock Lode of Nevada.* New York: Alfred A. Knopf, 1946.

Di Certo, Joseph. *The Saga of the Pony Express.* Missoula, MT: Mountain Press, 2002.

Egan, Ferol. *Sand in a Whirlwind: The Paiute Indian War of 1860.* New York: Doubleday, 1972.

Godfrey, Anthony, and Roy Webb. *Pony Express: The Story Behind the Scenery*. Las Vegas: KC Publications, 1999.

National Park Service. "The Pony Express: Historic Resource Study" 2008.

Reinfeld, Fred. *Pony Express*. Lincoln, NE: Bison Books, 1973

Rice, Edward. *Captain Sir Richard Francis Burton*. New York: Charles Scribner's Sons, 1990.

Settle, Raymond W., and Mary Lund Settle. *Saddles and Spurs: The Pony Express Saga*. Harrisburg, PA: Stackpole Books, 1955.

Skelton, Charles L. *Riding West on the Pony Express*. New York: Macmillan, 1937.

Twain, Mark. *Roughing It*. New York: New American Library, 1962.

Warren, Andrea. *The Boy Who Became Buffalo Bill. Growing Up Billy Cody in Bleeding Kansas*. New York: Two Lions, 2015.

Williams, George III. *Mark Twain: His Life in Virginia City, Nevada*. Dayton, NV: Tree By the River Publishing Co., 1990.

Questions for Discussion

1. Why do you think the history of the Pony Express remains so popular?

2. Why was the Pony Express important?

3. Would you like to have been a Pony Express rider? Why?

4. What forms of transportation did people use to travel west?

5. What did Mark Twain think of the Pony Express, and why were his memories important to its history?

6. What is left of the Pony Express route?

7. What horse breeds were used by the riders, and why were they chosen?

8. Was the Pony Express financially successful? If not, why not?

9. How did the conflict with the Paiute people impact the Pony Express?

10. Pretend you're a Pony Express rider. What would you see on the trail?

Index

bison 15, 23
Buckland's Station 35, 36, 38, 40
Buffalo Bill v, 53, 54, 55, 56, 57, 59, 60, 61, 71, 72, 73 *see also* Cody, W.
Buntline, Ned 55, 61, 72
Butterfield Overland Mail 9, 43, 70

Carson City, NV 1, 21, 29, 35, 37, 46, 47, 49, 52, 71, 72
Central Overland California & Pikes Peak Express Company 5, 19
Chorpenning, George, Jr. 8
Civil War vii, 9, 10, 40-42, 58, 61, 62, 66
Cody, William Frederick 53, 54, 55, 56, 58, 59, 60, 71, 72, 73
Congressional Medal of Honor 59

Davis, Nellie Mighels 47
DeQuille, Dan 48, 72

emigrants 7, 10, 15, 16, 40, 43

financial struggles 11, 12, 62
Fort Churchill 40, 42

Frye, Johnny 28, 31
Greeley, Horace 49, 50, 51, 71
Gwin, William 10, 11, 71

Hamilton, William 29, 30
Haslam, Robert 34-38, 40, 41, 42, 47, 48, 50, 67, 68, 71 *see also* Pony Bob
Hayes, Rutherford B. 52
hostlers 12, 13, 15

Jackass Mail vii, 8
James, William "Bill" 6, 28, 30, 32, 40, 45, 46, 71, 76

Keetley, Jack 32
Kelley, J.G. 32, 33, 38

Landis, Israel 21
The Land of Purple Shadows 48

Majors, Alexander vii, 10, 11, 13, 14, 16, 17, 19, 20, 53, 54, 58, 62, 63, 71
mochila 22, 30, 32, 38, 41, 70
Monk, Hank v, 43-52, 65, 71
Morgan horses 13, 70

Native Americans, struggle with 16, 24, 27, 33, 36-40
Numaga 37

Oakley, Annie 56, 57, 71
Ormsby, Major William 33, 36, 37

Paiute 16, 24, 32, 33, 35, 36, 37, 38, 39, 40, 41, 42, 70, 72, 74
Panama 6, 7, 46
Placerville, CA 29, 30, 46, 47, 49, 50, 71
Pony Bob v, 34, 38, 40, 41, 42, 47, 48, 66, 69, 71
postage 20
Pyramid Lake War 32, 37, 39

ranchers 15
Randall, James 30
relay stations 13, 33, 35, 36 *see also* swing stations
Richardson, J.W. "Billy" 28, 31, 38
Roberts, Bolivar 34, 35
Roff, Harry 30
Roughing It x, 49, 51, 73
route 1, 6, 7, 8, 11, 13, 17, 20, 23, 24, 30, 33, 34, 36, 38, 44, 46, 64, 68, 69, 70, 74
Russell, William vii, 10, 11, 12, 13, 14, 17, 19, 20, 53, 54, 60, 62, 63, 71

saddle 3, 5, 13, 16, 21, 22, 29, 32, 38, 42, 54, 68, 70
salary 17, 21

Sherman, William Tecumseh 52
Shoshone 8, 32, 70
Sierra Nevada 6, 8, 29, 42, 49, 50
stagecoach 1, 3, 36, 46, 50, 52, 65, 70
St. Joseph, MO vii, 2, 10, 11, 20, 21, 25, 30
Sutter's Mill vii, 6
swing stations 12, 13

Tate, Billy 33
telegraph vii, 8, 9, 42, 50, 61
Thompson, John "Snowshoe" 8
Thoroughbred horses 14, 15, 70
transcontinental railroad 44
Twain, Mark x, 4, 48, 49, 51, 60, 71, 73, 74

US Post Office 8
Utah Territory vii, 7, 8, 20, 29, 32, 44, 65, 70

Waddell, William vii, 10, 11, 13, 14, 19, 20, 53, 54, 62, 63, 71
Wells, Fargo & Co. 43, 46, 66, 67, 68
Wells Fargo Concord Coach 44, 45
Williams Station 36, 38
Woodward, Absolam 8

Young, Brigham 32

About the Author

Native Nevadan John L. Smith is a longtime journalist and the author of more than a dozen books including *Saints, Sinners, and Sovereign Citizens: The Endless War Over the West's Public Lands*. He has won many state, regional, and national awards for his writing and was inducted into the Nevada Press Association Newspaper Hall of Fame in 2016, the same year that saw him honored with the James Foley/Medill
Medal for Courage in Journalism, the Society of Professional Journalists Ethics Award, and the Ancil Payne Award for Ethics in Journalism from the University of Oregon. He freelances for a variety of publications, including *The Nevada Independent*. The father of a grown daughter, Amelia, he is married to the writer Sally Denton and makes his home in Boulder City, Nevada.

www.ingramcontent.com/pod-product-compliance
Lightning Source LLC
Chambersburg PA
CBHW062039120526
44592CB00035B/1655